Our
Wilderness
America's Common Ground

Doug Scott

Campaign for America's Wilderness

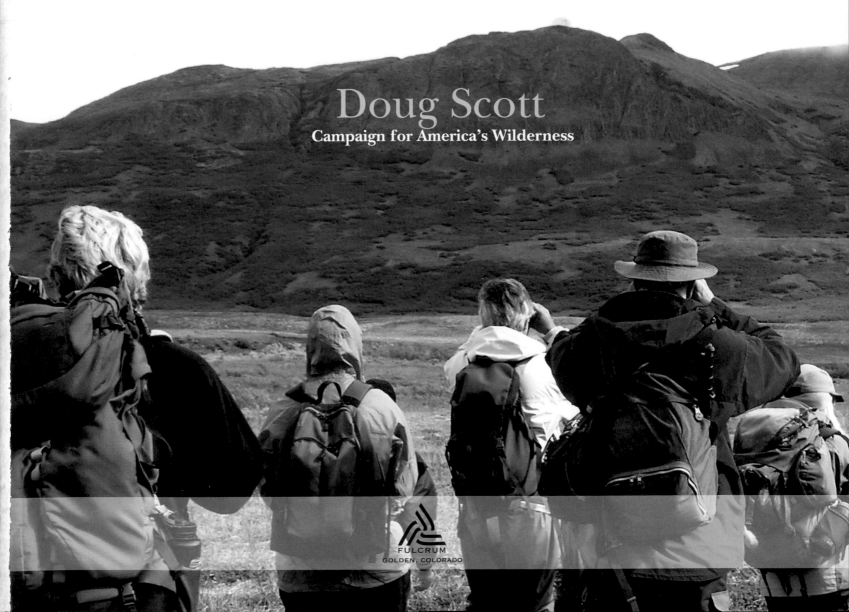

FULCRUM
GOLDEN, COLORADO

Library of Congress Cataloging-in-Publication
Data

Scott, Doug.
  Our wilderness : America's common ground
/ Doug Scott.
     p. cm.
  ISBN 978-1-55591-641-1 (pbk. : alk. paper)
1. Landscape photography--United States.
2. Wilderness areas--United States--Pictorial
works. I. Title.
  TR660.S39 2009
  333.78'2160973--dc22

                              2007029278

Printed in Canada by Friesens Corp.
0 9 8 7 6 5 4 3 2 1

Design: Jack Lenzo
Cover image: Proposed 20,000-acre Browns
Canyon Wilderness in south-central Colorado,
near Salida. © Jeff Widen
Title page: Katmai National Park and Preserve,
300 miles southwest of Anchorage, Alaska.
© Shutterstock

Fulcrum Publishing
4690 Table Mountain Drive, Suite 100
Golden, Colorado 80403
800-992-2908 • 303-277-1623
www.fulcrumbooks.com

Author's Note: All wilderness statistics and
references to "proposed wilderness" not
yet designated by Congress were current in
November 2008. For up-to-date statistics and
information on every designated wilderness
area, see www.wilderness.net. For the status
of proposed wilderness areas, visit
www.leaveitwild.org.

Every time I go there, it's like walking into heaven. There are no words to express that feeling. I love it.

—John Roskelly, famed Everest climber, describing the proposed Scotchman Peaks Wilderness (Idaho and Montana)

Our remnants of wilderness will yield bigger values to the nation's character and health than they will to its pocketbook, and to destroy them will be to admit that the latter are the only values that interest us.

—Aldo Leopold, "A Plea for Wilderness Hunting Grounds," *Outdoor Life*, November 1925

Wilderness touches something deep and fundamental in the American psyche. We have grown up with songs and images writ large on screens, in books, and as anthems about our precious natural heritage of wilderness majesty.

Despite impressive natural wonders such as Victoria Falls, the Alps, and the Amazon, nowhere can you find the incredible array of beautiful monuments of nature as in American wilderness areas. If they are to be sacrificed for short-term benefits by mining, drilling, and damming—especially for seeking profits from nonrenewable resources for our future energy—we will have squandered an incredible treasure.

Our frontier heritage did much to shape the idea of what it means to be American: pioneer values such as self-sufficiency and rugged individualism, community, and working together to find common ground.

And so it follows that what we choose to preserve defines us as a people and a society. Just as we strive always to protect the tenets of the Constitution and the Declaration of Independence, so too should we strive always to protect great wild places like the Great Smokies, the Grand Canyon, and Yellowstone—and we should do more to preserve other wild places such as the rain forests of southeast Alaska and the red rock canyon lands of southern Utah.

We preserve untamed wild places for adventure and recreation, as living classrooms to introduce our children to nature, as sanctuaries of quiet and solitude and peace. They should be left as nature shaped them, for every generation to enjoy.

In any list of the greatest laws our Congress has enacted is the 1964 Wilderness Act, the charter that guides preservation of unique and wild places on our public lands. It was passed and land continues to be protected because of the efforts of ordinary citizens who have pushed and prodded when necessary, and worked with public officials and members of Congress from both parties to see beloved landscapes preserved.

Still, too much of our public land faces relentless development pressures and lacks this highest form of protection. Inspired by this book, which tells the history of a good idea put into action by the democratic, bipartisan efforts of people just like you and me, we can get to work on ensuring that more of these last great places on Earth remain wild and pure and free.

[signature]

Take a walk with me

along this inviting trail, dappled with sunlight shimmering through the leafy canopy. Listen to the wind rustling in the trees, birdsong, water lapping in the creek along our path. With just a few bends of the trail, we've left behind the whine and clank of twenty-first-century machines.

Here, in wilderness, you can better hear your own heart. If you linger, you can begin to tune in to something deeper: the Earth's ancient pulse, to which all life on our planet evolves. And, amazing as it may seem, we are strolling in a wild haven of nature just a half day's drive from Washington, DC.

Join me for another hike,

but watch your footing: we're on hummocky, trail-less ground. Along this wild shoreline we may surprise a moose or brown bear, for we're exploring, glorying in a vast wilderness sanctuary in Alaska.

Climb the mountains and get their good tidings. Nature's peace will flow into you as sunshine flows into trees. The winds will blow their own freshness into you, and the storms their energy, while cares will drop off like autumn leaves. Like a generous host, she offers here brimming cups in endless variety, served in a grand hall, the sky its ceiling, the mountains its walls, decorated with glorious paintings and enlivened with bands of music ever playing.

—John Muir, *Our National Parks*

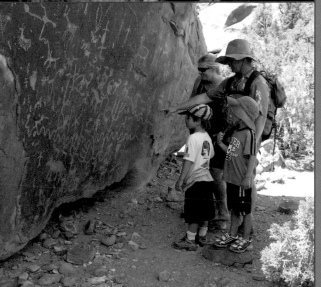

In these two walks, we've been in wilderness areas: first the Otter Creek Wilderness in West Virginia, then Katmai Wilderness, Alaska. Their preservation would not have been possible without one of our nation's most important conservation laws: the Wilderness Act of 1964.

In that law, Congress declared that it would preserve wilderness areas such as these in order to be sure that "an increasing population, accompanied by expanding settlement and growing mechanization, does not occupy and modify all areas within the United States and its possessions, leaving no lands designated for preservation and protection in their natural condition."

By the end of 2008, Congress had preserved more than seven hundred wilderness areas large and small, nearly 110 million acres, under the Wilderness Act. These wild sanctuaries—all part of the public lands we all share—embrace the geographical and biological diversity of our forests, mountains, wetlands, prairies, and coastlines. Together, they make up our growing National Wilderness Preservation System. While some wilderness areas are as remote as the peaks of Alaska or the Rockies, others come right to the city limits of Tucson or Salt Lake City. You can visit a wilderness area not far from your home: they are found in forty-four of the fifty states, and Puerto Rico.

Nearly every year Congress extends wilderness protection to additional parts of our wildest public lands. They do so because Americans overwhelmingly support this work and because ordinary citizens who love a particular wild place work with their elected representatives to obtain the legislation needed. Why Congress and citizens do this is pretty simple: because we humans need these wild retreats, places where the cacophony of our mechanized, technological civilization does not drown out the wild symphonies of the natural world. And because so many of us—and our senators, representatives, and presidents—understand our responsibility to leave a living legacy of wild America for all the generations to come.

The wilderness concept was created by people, for people.
People are welcome in these quiet sanctuaries; only machinery is out of place
(but allowed in some other parts of our public lands). While these wild havens
offer diverse outdoor recreational opportunities, perhaps their greatest value is
as living museums and classrooms where we may better understand our place in
the natural world, how nature is the very foundation of our human culture.

We never outgrow the fact that human cultures arose in utter dependence on the land and its bounty. Like native peoples and pioneers before us, we can discover anew the meaning of self-sufficiency and independence in wilderness areas. In wilderness, we can leave behind for a time the cares and the accumulations of our twenty-first-century lives and return to things more natural, not the least being a sense of our ties to the earth and connectedness to the natural world.

Wilderness is not—and should not be—a past and vanishing force in American life. It is, as far as anyone can see into the future in our rapidly changing and uncertain world, an abiding value—a necessity not only for the good life, but for life itself.

—George Marshall, former president, Sierra Club

Some of us choose to view wilderness from afar,

in a book or on film. Others walk into the wilderness, clicking a shutter or stalking a wily trout or elk. Some climb a ridge or a peak to camp far beyond the end of the road, while others only daydream about such adventures.

Riders test their horseback skills on wilderness trails. Birders delight in discovering elusive species new to their life lists. Others record their wild inspirations in a journal or on canvas, challenged to capture in their own way the splendors of a vast wilderness scene or the close observation of a wild mountain flower. Parents and grandparents share nature at its wildest with a child, thrilled at how even the youngest is enchanted by the beauties of God's original creation.

In wilderness, you can hone your outdoor skills, reflect on your place in the natural world, face challenge and risk, or just relax.

Here, perhaps better than anywhere, you can learn new things about yourself. However you choose to enjoy wilderness, it is the setting for wild, life-enriching discovery.

12

Those who contemplate the beauty of the earth find reserves of strength that will endure as long as life lasts... **There is something infinitely healing in the repeated refrains of nature** —the assurance that dawn comes after night, and spring after winter. The lasting pleasures of contact with the natural world are not reserved for scientists but are available to anyone who will place himself under the influence of earth, sea, and sky, and their amazing life.

—Rachel Carson, *The Sense of Wonder*

[We have] preserved for now and for generations unborn, areas of unspoiled wilderness, accessible by a system of trails, unmarred by roads or buildings, but open to use and enjoyment of hikers, mountain climbers, hunters, fishermen, and trail riders, and of all those who find, in high and lonely places, a refreshment of the spirit, and life's closest communion with God.

—Senator Frank Church, as the US Senate passed the Wilderness Act, 1961

[The] real function [of wilderness] will always be as a spiritual backlog in the high-speed mechanical world in which we live. We have discovered that the presence of wilderness in itself is a balance wheel and an aid to equilibrium.

—Sigurd F. Olson, nature writer

In God's wilderness lies the hope of the world…Whether as seen carving the lines of the mountains with glaciers, or gathering matter into stars, or planning the movements of water,—still all is Beauty!

—John Muir, unpublished journals

My family tree has deep roots in this land; ten generations of my West Virginia ancestors passed down an abiding respect for nature that is based on my faith. In wilderness, I feel God's creation, in its silence, God's majesty. In wilderness, I find peace. It's our responsibility to preserve this wilderness—its clean air and water, fish and wildlife, and amazing wild forests—so that our children and grandchildren will be blessed with the beauty of God's creation too.

—Carol Warren, resident, Potato Knob, West Virginia

Wild beauty inspires art,

music, and literature. Throughout our history, poets and artists have been drawn to the wildest places in the American landscape. The art that emerges from such wilderness encounters attracts us in an almost visceral way. Think of how an Ansel Adams photo naturally grasps your attention. Listen to *Appalachian Spring* and you hear not just folk tunes, but the deeper echo of the wild mountain settings from which they sprang.

Famed painter Thomas Cole captured that essence, writing in 1835 that "the most distinctive, and perhaps the most impressive, characteristic of American scenery is its wildness." Cole's idea resonates with anyone who has aimed a camera, taken up a drawing pad, or sought, in verse or journal, to capture his or her personal response to a sweeping wilderness vista or the beauty of a tiny wild blossom.

Whether gazing into the wild from a roadside picnic area or immersed in it on a weeklong outing, here artificial, man-made influences fade as our senses and creativity find stimulus in what is utterly, wildly natural. Frank Lloyd Wright sought nature "every day for inspiration in the day's work. I follow in building the principles which nature has used in its domain." Painter Maxfield Parrish wrote of the inspiration he found "up in this northern wilderness" near his home in New Hampshire: "There seem to be magic days once in a while, with some rare quality of light that hold a body spellbound…there will be a burst of unbelievable color when the mountain turns a deep purple."

Even if you never set foot in wilderness,

observing wilderness and wildlife from a road or developed picnic site can be the experience of a lifetime. Though many Americans enter wilderness areas to enjoy their wonders up close, many more are drawn to the edges of wilderness to glory in its wild scenic beauty.

People want to be close to nature, to live with wilderness areas on their horizon. More and more Americans choose to live in rural places, often near national forests or other federal lands, to enjoy the abundant recreational opportunities they offer. For others, it is enough to look up from the deck or the kitchen counter at sweeping vistas of nature—the wilder the better.

We simply need that wild country available to us, even if we never do more than drive to its edge and look in. For it can be a means of reassuring ourselves of our sanity as creatures, a part of the geography of hope.

—Wallace Stegner, *The Sound of Mountain Water*

The very existence of wilderness adds quality to what surrounds it and to what people experience as they merely look inside…Wilderness adds quality in roadside scenery. Wilderness lets a place have a beyond to it. Wilderness symbolizes the freedom to choose what kinds of terrain you want to look at, or hope someday to enter or to save for your children to enter.

—David R. Brower, first executive director, Sierra Club

We need the tonic of wildness,—to wade sometimes in marshes where the bittern and the meadow-hen lurk, and hear the booming of the snipe. We can never have enough of nature. We must be refreshed by the sight of inexhaustible vigor, vast and titanic features...the wilderness with its living and its decaying trees, the thunder-cloud, and the rain which lasts three weeks and produces freshets. We need to witness our own limits transgressed, and some life pasturing freely where we never wander.

—Henry David Thoreau, *Walden*

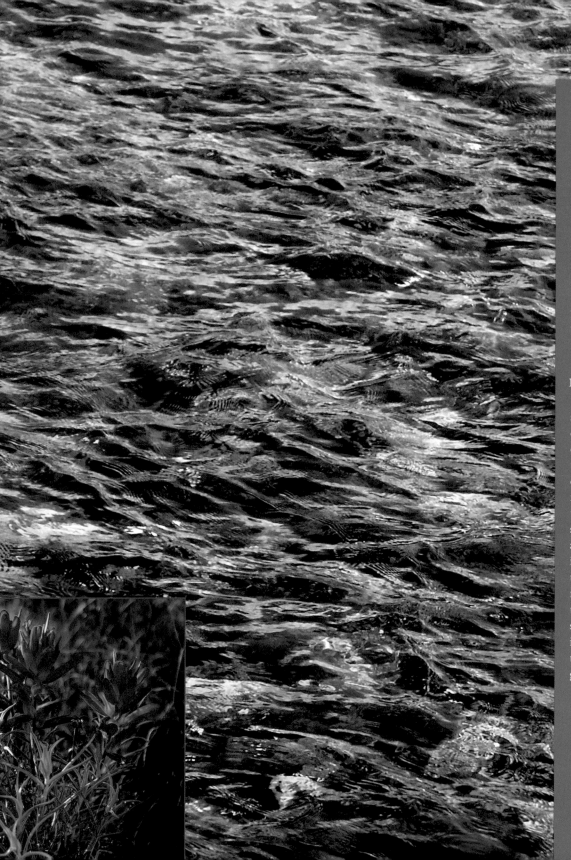

Of the many values wilderness offers, none is more important than stimulating our understanding of the natural world, on a small as well as a large scale. In wilderness areas we protect the natural communities of plants and animals, including threatened and endangered species. Here wildflowers bloom in dazzling displays and wildlife can be found "pasturing freely," in Thoreau's phrase—including species such as spawning salmon (pictured here), mountain goats, elk, woodpeckers, wolverine, and grizzlies, which require large, undisturbed habitats to survive. Thus, preserving wilderness areas helps maintain life-sustaining biodiversity. Wilderness areas are reservoirs of clean air, while wilderness watersheds protect fountains of clean water so economically vital to downstream farmers, towns, and cities. Scientific studies in these most natural "living laboratories" help track the condition of our planet, affording scientists undisturbed benchmarks against which to assess humans' impacts in more-developed areas. In the final analysis, preserving wilderness is not only a responsibility we owe to future generations, but may also someday be seen as one of the most important contributions our generation could make to the health of our global environment.

21

The chief biologic and economic reason for preserving wilderness areas is...that they are great reservoirs of the serene order of nature, where things work the way they ought to. They are the right answers in the back of the book, from which we can get help in solving our problems outside them...

—Donald Culross Peattie, botanist and author

Friend of Wilderness: Jean Craighead George

Few have influenced more Americans' appreciation of nature than Jean Craighead George. Among her more than one hundred books, the classic *Julie of the Wolves* won the 1973 Newbery Medal and *My Side of the Mountain* was a 1960 Newbery Honor Book.

"Children are still in love with the wonders of nature, and I am too. So I tell them stories about a boy and a falcon, a girl and an elegant wolf pack, about owls, weasels, foxes, prairie dogs, the alpine tundra, the tropical rain forest. And when the telling is done, I hope they will want to protect all the beautiful creatures and places. I'm not lecturing and telling children to go out and save the wilderness. I want them to come to love them so much that they realize that they must save them."

Recalling a Wyoming wilderness outing with one of her children, George writes that "it was as if a door had closed behind us, and there was such peace of mind along that trail that I have never found anywhere else. Just to remove the clutter from our life for two days and sit there with a child you love is an experience that lasts for years and years.

"I'll never go to some of these wonderful wilderness areas, but I want to know they're there and I think most people do. It's important to the spirit of every American to keep the wilderness intact."

24

Visiting wilderness areas, we are reminded of the deep influence the wilderness frontier played in our history. Here you may trace age-old Indian trading trails, the route of Lewis and Clark, the pathways of Spanish conquistadors, or the ruts of pioneer wagons across the prairie grasslands. In wilderness, you can walk in the footsteps of Daniel Boone or paddle a canoe or kayak in the historic wake of LaSalle and the voyageurs. **Wilderness is about Americans' history of living with this land.**

Protecting wilderness also helps preserve the archaeological record—not just specific archaeological sites, but the wild surroundings that were integral to those cultures. A crumbling chimney or a long-overgrown orchard recalls the lives of early homesteaders.

Where still visible in wilderness areas, the marks of old logging or mining sites and roads are fading too, offering fascinating lessons of the restorative powers of nature at work. In writing the Wilderness Act, Congress named history as one value in preserving wilderness areas and deliberately avoided requiring that only areas untouched by man could be protected.

But just as we need wilderness,

it needs us. These quiet wilderness solitudes cannot save themselves. It takes an act of Congress to extend the legal protection of the 1964 Wilderness Act to additional areas. For more than four decades, many thousands of ordinary people have spoken up to help protect wilderness, their voices leading Congress to pass the laws that preserved these special places. As the Montana Wilderness Association succinctly puts it, "Wilderness is protected by citizen action, not by accident."

To understand the story of our American wilderness, we must consider not only the many values people have for preserving it—the *why*—but the ways in which these areas have, in fact, been saved—the *how* and the *who*. It makes for an inspiring story.

We are part of the wilderness of the universe. That is our nature. Our noblest, happiest character develops with the influence of wildness…With the wilderness we are at home. Some of us think we see this so clearly that for ourselves, for our children, our continuing posterity, and our fellow men we covet with a consuming intensity the fullness of the human development that keeps its contact with wildness. Out of the wilderness, we realize, has come the substance of our culture, and with a living wilderness—it is our faith—we shall have also a vibrant culture, an enduring civilization of healthful citizens who renew themselves when they are in contact with the earth.

—Howard Zahniser, author of the Wilderness Act

Before people could think about preserving wilderness, **they had to view areas of wild nature as worth saving.** For thousands of years in Western culture, wilderness was a fearsome place—and a fearsome idea. Dark woods beyond the stockade or town walls were places of unspeakable dangers. The goal of civilization was to vanquish wilderness, not cherish it.

By contrast, indigenous hunting-and-gathering societies, such as American Indians and Alaska Natives, saw themselves as part of the natural world. Chief Luther Standing Bear of the Ogalala Sioux explained that his people "did not think of the great open plains, the beautiful rolling hills, and the winding streams with their tangled growth as 'wild.' Only to the white man was nature a 'wilderness' and…the land 'infested with wild animals and savage people.'"

The earliest European settlers brought with them to North America all the age-old fears of wilderness. But new ideas were stirring. Influenced by European romanticism, American painters and poets began to celebrate wild nature precisely because it was wild. Ideas of the sublimity of nature generated in the English Lake District and the Alps applied equally well to the Adirondacks and the Northwoods. Thomas Cole, Frederic Edwin Church, and their fellow painters of the Hudson River School celebrated pastoral landscapes but increasingly turned to even wilder scenes. It was an idea shared by poets, such as William Cullen Bryant, and novelists, including James Fenimore Cooper in his wildly popular *Leatherstocking Tales*. In their widely read essays, Ralph Waldo Emerson and Henry David Thoreau found God's own handiwork in undefiled nature.

To him who in the love of Nature holds
Communion with her visible forms, she speaks
A various language; for his gayer hours
She has a voice of gladness, and a smile
And eloquence of beauty, and she glides
Into his darker musings, with a mild
And healing sympathy, that steals away
Their sharpness, ere he is aware.

—William Cullen Bryant, "Thanotopsis"

Opposite: Artist Thomas Cole pointing out a wilderness scene to poet William Cullen Bryant, as depicted in this tribute by their friend, artist Asher B. Durand, *Kindred Spirits*, 1849, oil on canvas, 44" x 36", Courtesy Crystal Bridges Museum of American Art, Bentonville, Arkansas

Venturing to the West with early explorers, painters Albert Bierstadt and Thomas Moran celebrated the remarkable wild scenery of the Sierras and Rockies. Their art helped in the campaigns to preserve Yosemite and Yellowstone national parks. Moran's western adventures were sometimes in company with military explorations, which increasingly employed photographers whose images were widely published. As wilderness historian Roderick Nash reports, Congress appropriated $10,000 in 1874 for one of Moran's wilderness paintings to hang in the lobby of the US Senate and thus "the American wilderness received official endorsement as a subject for national pride."

Contrasted to the civilized environment of the Old World, our wilderness was something unique around which Americans could marshal patriotic pride. In the mid-eighteenth century, painter and essayist Charles Lanman enthused, "A fig for your Italian scenery!…this is the land to study nature in all her luxuriant charms…to feel your soul expand under the mighty influences of nature in her primitive beauty and strength!"

In this way, our wilderness became a part of Americans' fundamental sense of who we are as a people.

I used to envy the father of our race, dwelling as he did in contact with the new-made fields and plants of Eden; but I do so no more, because I have discovered that I also live in "creation's dawn." The morning stars still sing together, and the world, not yet half made, becomes more beautiful every day.

—John Muir, *John of the Mountains*

President Theodore Roosevelt and John Muir on the rim of Yosemite Valley, 1903

As pioneers crossed the continent, taming the wilderness on a massive scale, there was great waste—bison herds exterminated, forests scalped in a sorry history of cut-and-move-on logging. But increasingly, voices were heard not only demanding wiser use of natural resources, but urging that some wild lands be saved.

John Muir popularized the national park idea and helped found the Sierra Club in 1872. Ideals of conserving our natural resources were championed from the bully pulpit of the White House by President Theodore Roosevelt. "We have gotten past the stage, my fellow citizens," said Roosevelt, standing at the rim of the Grand Canyon in 1903, "when we are to be pardoned if we simply treat any part of our country as something to be skinned for two or three years for the use of the present generation. Whether it is the forest, the water, the scenery, whatever it is, handle it so that your children's children will get the benefit of it."

In the 1920s, Aldo Leopold, a young US Forest Service official working in the Southwest, began promoting the idea that we should deliberately set apart wilderness areas to protect some federal lands from the onslaught of roads and motors. Thanks to his leadership, the Gila Wilderness Area, New Mexico, became the world's first official wilderness area, in 1924. The idea caught on. In 1935, Leopold, Bob Marshall, and others founded The Wilderness Society to further spread the wilderness preservation idea.

Aldo Leopold, 1924

We abuse land because we regard it as a commodity belonging to us. When we see land as a community to which we belong, we may begin to use it with love and respect.

—Aldo Leopold, *A Sand County Almanac*

Howard Zahniser

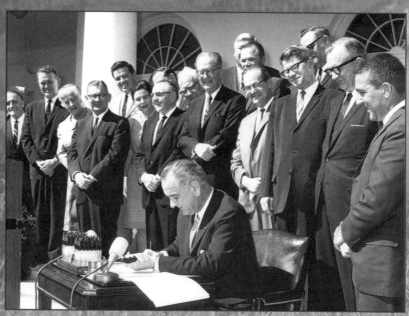

President Johnson signs the Wilderness Act, 1964

By 1939, the US Forest Service had used administrative protection orders to establish more than seventy national forest wilderness areas totaling 14 million acres. Along with these and other still-unprotected roadless areas in the national forests, conservation leaders viewed the wild, undeveloped backcountry of national parks and national wildlife refuges as desirable parts of a nationwide system of wilderness areas. But none was adequately protected from creeping development that would destroy the wild character of the land. Even in the relatively few officially designated areas there was no real commitment that wilderness qualities would be preserved in perpetuity. As easily as they had been issued, administrative protection orders could be altered by the stroke of a pen. Agency administrators were free to trim back boundaries to make way for incremental developments—and did—all too easily nibbling away the wilderness.

Leaders of America's conservation organizations soon saw the need for some stronger kind of protection so they would not forever be on the defensive, fighting off one threat to wilderness lands after another— logging one place, dam-building another, and new roads seemingly being pushed up every wild valley. A wilderness law would give teeth to the idea that wilderness areas would, in fact, be preserved forever.

Howard Zahniser, the executive director of The Wilderness Society in the years after World War II, was the leader in this thinking. Beginning in the late 1940s, he began to work out ideas regarding what a wilderness law might do, consulting other leaders to carefully build groundwork for the strong coalition of conservation organizations whose support would be needed to pass such a law through Congress.

After nearly a decade of these preparations, the first wilderness preservation legislation was introduced in Congress in 1956. From the outset, it enjoyed bipartisan support, the lead sponsors a liberal Democrat in the Senate and a conservative Republican in the House of Representatives. Congressional deliberations continued for eight years, but ultimately public support and strong leadership from Presidents John F. Kennedy and Lyndon B. Johnson propelled the legislation to success. On September 3, 1964, members of Congress from both political parties gathered around President Johnson as he signed the Wilderness Act into law.

Those who advocate preserving additional wilderness areas feel an urgency to protect wild places still vulnerable to ill-considered road-building and encroachment by ever-increasing development. Even in 1937, when there still was so much wild land, wilderness champion Bob Marshall warned, "Wilderness is melting away like some last snowbank on some south-facing mountainside during a hot afternoon in June. It is disappearing while most of those who care more for it than anything else in the world are trying desperately to rally and save it."

Today, more than two-thirds of the unprotected federal lands that were roadless in 1940 have been touched, in some way, by development. Yes, Congress has preserved more wilderness over the years, but much has been lost, and there is more to be protected still.

This is our children's last chance too. So much has been used in our short past; so little is left for the long future. Our ability to keep wilderness alive in our days will be the measure of what we have learned from the history of man's abuse of the land—and as our children appraise the history we are writing, no harm will come from our decision to be generous in saving their wilderness.

—David R. Brower, first executive director, Sierra Club

Friend of Wilderness: Nancy Hall

When Nancy Hall moved to Mesquite, Nevada, she found work as a waitress. Soon she was exploring the nearby Mormon Mountains. Seeing this favorite wild place being invaded by off-road vehicles, she decided to get involved.

Before long, Nancy was hiking into the area with her congressional representatives' staff members, showing what would be lost if a proposed road were to cut through a slot canyon lined with pictographs. "You learn a lot about the power of ordinary citizenship when you put yourself out there," Hall says, reflecting on her pride when, at the end of 2004, President George W. Bush signed the law that protected "her" new 157,938-acre Mormon Mountains Wilderness.

"I had fun with it, getting more people to speak up," she says. "It's my special place. When I saw the growing threats to this fragile wilderness, I wasn't about to let anything hold me back."

The growth of our National Wilderness Preservation System is an inspiring story of American democracy at work,

of ordinary people motivated by the love of some wild place rolling up their sleeves to get involved as citizen advocates.

David Brower of the Sierra Club explained the motivation this way: "You like wilderness, let us suppose, and you want to see some of it saved… Real wilderness, big wilderness—country big enough to have a beyond to it and an inside. With space enough to separate you from the buzz, bang, screech, ring, yammer, and roar of the 24-hour commercial you wish hard your life would not be."

So you find other people who care about that special place too. Together, you get out on the trail to learn more about the area and begin to choose boundaries for a citizen wilderness proposal. You go to meetings with local officials who administer this federal land, to exchange information and get involved in their planning processes. And you find yourself working side by side with veterans of successful wilderness protection campaigns.

Of course, other people may have different ideas about the best use of this land, so there can be controversy. Yet instead of fighting, people with differing views may sit down—or get out on the trail together—to see if they can find common ground. Compromise is a part of the process.

So there you are, learning how decisions really get made in our federal government, and it can be an inspiring experience. It's inspiring because it illuminates the power of citizens in our democracy.

Ordinary people, from every imaginable walk of life (an orchardist, a hardware dealer, a cocktail waitress, a veteran), able-bodied and disabled, young and old, have been leaders in protecting wilderness areas. Each emerges with a hugely deepened appreciation of the workings of our democracy because they've joined in the political process to preserve land they love.

For many decades, wilderness advocates worked to protect wilderness in Alaska, the Great Land. Here, in America's greatest reservoir of wild lands, they felt wilderness should be preserved on a scale fitting this matchless landscape.

[Wilderness provides] a place to contemplate and try to understand our place in the world, an antidote to the confused state of mankind's mind in this atomic age.

—Olaus Murie, early advocate for Alaska wilderness protection

Alaska is huge, and all of it—375 million acres—was once federally owned. When Alaska joined the Union in 1959, Congress made a gift of more than a quarter of the land to the new state, allowing it to cherry-pick the most valuable land, such as Prudhoe Bay. In 1971, Congress settled long-standing claims of aboriginal owner-ship, conveying 44 million acres to Alaska's native peoples.

Fueled by the North Slope oil discovery, in the 1970s, Alaska, once derided as "Seward's Icebox," was like a gigantic pie of natural resources. Special interests were eagerly compet-ing to slice up the remaining federal land for development. Conservation-ists pleaded with Congress to dedicate some of the remaining federal lands for conservation as wildlife refuges, national parks, and wilderness. The idea caught on like wildfire.

45

To adopt a conservation plan for the federal lands in Alaska was an undertaking unmatched in conservation annals. America's outdoor and environmental organizations mobilized their largest grassroots lobbying campaign. The advocate-in-chief was Jimmy Carter, who made this bipartisan legislation a top priority of his presidency.

On December 2, 1980, President Carter lifted his pen to sign one of history's most sweeping conservation laws, the Alaska National Interest Lands Conservation Act. In a single stroke he doubled the size of our National Park System, our National Wild and Scenic Rivers System, our National Wildlife Refuge System, and our National Wilderness Preservation System—104 million acres in all.

President Jimmy Carter and his wife, Rosalynn, on a 1990 trip to the Arctic National Wildlife Refuge

As long as any of us serve in this House, we will cast no more important conservation votes than the votes on this Alaska lands bill. The simple fact is that Alaska...is our last chance to go about the job of conservation...with forethought, before a pattern of development has been fixed across the landscape piecemeal.

—Representative Morris K. Udall, as the
US House passed the Alaska Lands Act

By itself, the Alaska Lands Act stood as a ringing validation of the best of what the conservation movement has stood for in the century since Henry David Thoreau had walked so thoughtfully in the woods of Walden Pond.

—T. H. Watkins, historian

Wilderness Volunteer: Judy Mitchell

In one recent year, more than two hundred volunteers performed 5,500 hours of work in three wilderness areas in the Cascades of central Oregon—and had a great, safe time doing it, thanks to the leadership of the local volunteer coordinator, Judy Mitchell (left).

Her hometown newspaper introduced readers to Judy this way: "Meet a 66-year-old former nun who spends her days drawing a cross-cut saw over downed trees—sans pay—so people half her age can have access to trails in the Three Sisters Wilderness." Judy, who retired after eighteen years as a wilderness manager for the Forest Service, plans annual three-day training programs, then organizes volunteer parties who work surveying, marking, and maintaining trails, among other tasks. On a typical trip—with their gear carried by llamas, another passion of Judy's—she and five other volunteers cut thirty downed trees to clear five miles of trail.

"The trails we cleared could not have been cleared if we didn't do it," she said. "This is a great way for people of all ages and backgrounds to get out, do some healthy work, have a great time—and be of real service as stewards of our priceless wilderness heritage."

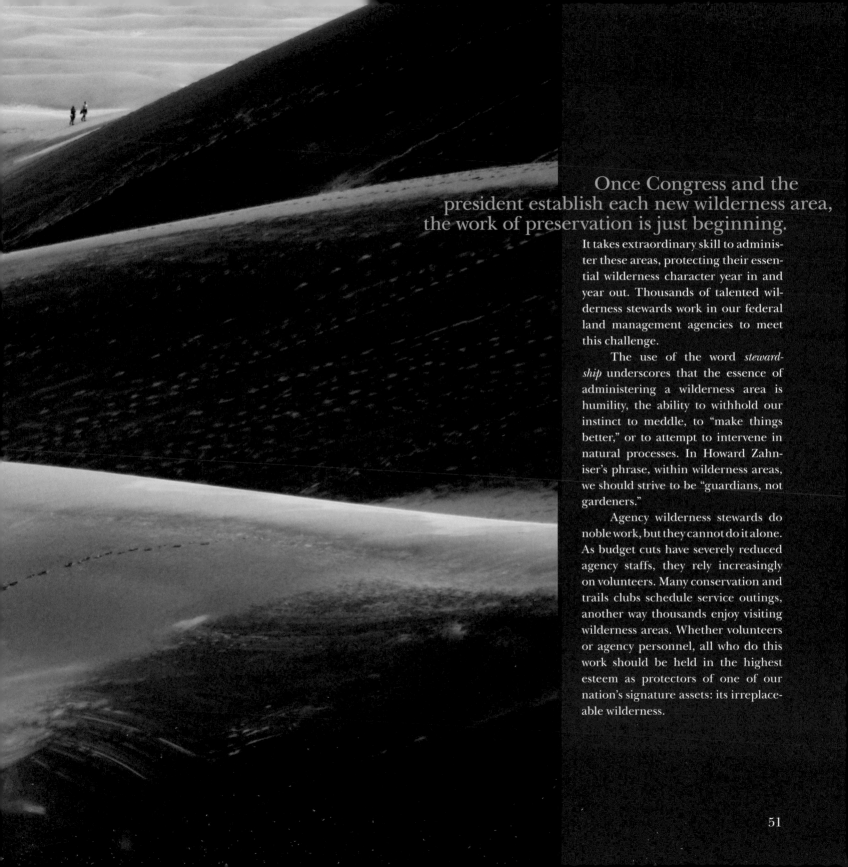

Once Congress and the president establish each new wilderness area, the work of preservation is just beginning.

It takes extraordinary skill to administer these areas, protecting their essential wilderness character year in and year out. Thousands of talented wilderness stewards work in our federal land management agencies to meet this challenge.

The use of the word *stewardship* underscores that the essence of administering a wilderness area is humility, the ability to withhold our instinct to meddle, to "make things better," or to attempt to intervene in natural processes. In Howard Zahniser's phrase, within wilderness areas, we should strive to be "guardians, not gardeners."

Agency wilderness stewards do noble work, but they cannot do it alone. As budget cuts have severely reduced agency staffs, they rely increasingly on volunteers. Many conservation and trails clubs schedule service outings, another way thousands enjoy visiting wilderness areas. Whether volunteers or agency personnel, all who do this work should be held in the highest esteem as protectors of one of our nation's signature assets: its irreplaceable wilderness.

One need not go to the center of a primitive area to enjoy it. Where does such an area begin? It begins where the road ends; and if the roads never end, there never will be any wilderness.

—Senator Frank Church, as the US Senate passed the Wilderness Act

Parks and Refuges: Reservoirs of Wilderness

When you visit a national park, perhaps Yosemite, you probably stop to view the famous sights and visit the rustic park lodge. But the focal point of your park visit is likely to be something else: the wilderness scenery that begins just beyond the edge of roads and developed tourist sites. Perhaps you've stopped at a pullout in Yellowstone to watch a bison or grizzly, or along Trail Ridge Road in Rocky Mountain National Park to see the elk, the whole scene enlivened as you observe the animals not in a zoo, but in their wilderness habitat.

When Congress established Yellowstone as the world's first national park in 1872, it set aside not just geysers and a canyon, but the surrounding 2 million acres—the whole vast natural setting. They were thinking in wilderness terms. The undeveloped wilderness beyond the roads furnishes the setting and the background that offers a large part of the pleasure of every visitor.

Today, the Wilderness Act protects the wildest parts of our national parks and national wildlife, carefully defining by law the wild zones that will not be whittled away or diluted by future development.

Growth and accelerating development are rapidly encroaching on open countryside, bringing unprecedented pressures for development to the very edge of wilderness and other public lands. Cities and their exurbs spread ever farther into what were once wide-open spaces. People are moving in huge numbers into rural places, such as the valleys in the Rocky Mountain states, to enjoy a simpler kind of life amid scenic beauty. Often there are unforeseen costs of this rush for development, loss of the very qualities people moved there to find: clean air and water, abundant wildlife, outdoor recreational opportunity—and nearby wild land.

Where wilderness has not yet been securely preserved, the pressures of this burgeoning human development may quickly become ungovernable.

As our population becomes greater, as industrial and other pressures close around the areas of wilderness still remaining, the necessity becomes greater...[to] preserve these buffers for the human spirit, seeing that they may long endure for the recreational, scientific, and historical uses of the American people.

—Representative John P. Saylor,
as he introduced the first
wilderness legislation, 1956

Today, communities such as Las Cruces, New Mexico, and Hood River, Oregon, are working to protect nearby wilderness using the power of the Wilderness Act to secure what they understand are vital community assets. Open spaces, accessible trails, and nearby wilderness recreational opportunities are increasingly recognized as hallmarks of communities offering a high quality of life.

My grandfather bought this land in 1910... Today, my wife and I grow pears and hay, and raise cattle. We've seen how, just in recent years, our region has lost a tremendous amount of wilderness and farmland to development. Only with permanent wilderness protection today can places that were special to me as a kid still be wild and free for kids tomorrow.

—Mike McCarthy, orchardist,
Hood River Valley, Oregon

The vast open spaces that surround Las Cruces truly define what makes our community and New Mexico unique. These special places are what attract record numbers of visitors...it just makes good sense to protect the wilderness we have.

—Carolyn Kuhn and John Vasquez, city
leaders, Las Cruces, New Mexico

Friend of Wilderness: Sandy Compton

A third-generation resident of rural northwestern Montana, Sandy Compton literally grew up in the shadow of wild peaks that are haunts of the reclusive mountain goat and grizzly. A writer and jack-of-all-trades, he has thought deeply about why he is working to protect the proposed Scotchman Peaks Wilderness that straddles the Idaho/Montana line in sight of his home.

"We humans are tamers of wild things," he reflects. "But if there are no wild places left in the world, where will we go to find the peace of silence? Where will we go to hear ourselves think? Where will we go to meet with God?"

A Final Word for the Wild

It is common for us to think of our public lands as a bountiful cornucopia of useful natural resources we can harvest: timber, water, game animals and fish, minerals, oil and gas, forage for grazing livestock.

But we Americans, so blessed to have vast public lands, have come to value them for another natural resource—the natural resource of silence, of the opportunity for solitude, for reconnecting to the natural community of all life.

Philosophers and naturalists have written volumes about the values we gain, individually and as a society, from keeping ourselves well grounded and in touch with the natural world. Political leaders have voiced these ideas too. Republican representative John Saylor of Pennsylvania told his colleagues as he first unveiled the proposed Wilderness Act in 1956, "The stress and strain of our crowded, fast-moving, highly-mechanized and raucously noisy civilization create another great need for wilderness—a deep need for areas of solitude and quiet, for areas of wilderness where life has not yet given way to machinery."

Preserving our wilderness is an act of supreme humility. It is an offering of restraint, a conscious decision to withhold all the man-made change and impact we *could* so easily spread everywhere across our landscape, utterly isolating ourselves—and future generations—from the original land.

Furthermore, preserving wilderness—America's common ground—is an act of generosity to all the future, a vote in favor of generations unborn, the offering of a living, wild legacy.

Solitude...is essential to any depth of meditation or character; and solitude in the presence of natural beauty and grandeur, is the cradle of thoughts and aspirations which are not only good for the individual, but which society could ill do without.

—John Stuart Mill, philosopher

Primer: What Is a Wilderness Area?

The Wilderness Act chartered our National Wilderness Preservation System to comprise wild portions of national forests, national parks, and other federal lands. Only Congress can establish wilderness areas, giving their boundaries the protection of statutory law.

1. There are more than 2.2 billion acres of land in the United States. Two-thirds is privately owned. Of the remainder, 630 million acres are federal conservation lands. These public lands are comprised of:

- National forests and grasslands administered by the US Forest Service
- National parks and preserves protected by the National Park Service
- National wildlife refuges managed by the US Fish and Wildlife Service
- Vast expanses of rangeland, desert, and forest in the West administered by the Bureau of Land Management

Much of our federal land has been made available for development—for logging, mining, dams and reservoirs, roads, campgrounds, and other tourism facilities.

2. Thanks to the 1964 Wilderness Act, Congress can decide to protect selected portions of federal conservation lands as wilderness. (Some states also protect wilderness areas on their state-owned lands.)

3. It takes a law passed by Congress and signed by the president to protect each area of federal land under the Wilderness Act. Since 1964, Congress has passed more than 130 laws establishing additional wilderness areas, often including several areas in a single law. In the Wilderness Act, Congress promised to preserve these areas as "an enduring resource of wilderness…for the permanent good of the whole people."

4. Statutory wilderness designation by act of Congress is the strongest protection we can give wild lands. Congress specifies a detailed boundary map as part of the law establishing each wilderness area. Once protected by law, it takes majorities of both the US Senate and House of Representatives and the approval of the president—that is, the passage of a new law—to alter a wilderness boundary or weaken its protection.

5. When Congress designates an area as wilderness, it is adding an additional layer of protection for that land, requiring the administering agency to preserve its wilderness character. This does not change which agency administers the land: the US Forest Service is responsible for stewardship of our national forest wilderness areas, the National Park Service for wilderness portions of our national parks, and so on. Thus, the four federal conservation agencies share in protecting our National Wilderness Preservation System.

6. Some wilderness areas (or several that adjoin each other) are very large, measuring millions of acres in an unbroken expanse. Others are very small—the smallest is a five-acre island. Our national treasury of wilderness areas embraces mountain peaks, deserts, deep forests, grasslands, swamps, and islands. It reflects the natural diversity of America.

What You Can Do in Wilderness Areas
- Hike, backpack, camp
- Canoe, kayak, raft
- Fish
- Cross-country ski, snowshoe
- Study nature
- Photograph, paint, draw
- Ride horses and enjoy pack trips
- Use wheelchairs (including certain motorized wheelchairs)
- Enjoy commercial guiding and outfitting services
- Hunt (except in national park wilderness)

What You Cannot Do in Wilderness Areas
- Ride motorized vehicles (dirt bikes, ATVs, snowmobiles)
- Ride mechanical vehicles (mountain bikes)

Resource Uses Prohibited in Wilderness Areas
- Logging
- Road building (except for firefighting)
- Establishing new mining claims
- Building new dams, reservoirs, power lines, pipelines
- Drilling for oil and gas, mining (but see the following)

Private Rights and Preestablished Privileges That Are Protected*
- Livestock grazing privileges held by local ranchers
- Private owners' continued use of private lands where surrounded by wilderness, with reasonable access assured
- Mining on valid, preexisting claims or on private lands
- Oil and gas drilling on valid, preexisting mineral leases

* Where established at the time each wilderness area was designated by Congress

Wilderness Facts

- Today, our national wilderness system embraces nearly 110 million acres (as of 2008).
- More than seven hundred wilderness areas, large and small, exhibit the geographical and biological diversity of the original American landscape.
- Less than 3 percent of all the land in our country outside of Alaska has this legal protection.
- Even when you add the huge wilderness areas in Alaska, just 5 percent of all of the land in America is currently preserved as wilderness.
- Congress continues the work of choosing new federal lands for wilderness protection "for the permanent good of the whole people."

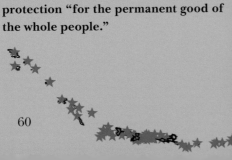

• Wilderness areas east of the Rockies are fewer and smaller only because there is less federal land there. Congress continues to add additional parts of eastern national forests, national parks, and national wildlife refuges to assure ample wilderness remains available close to so much of the nation's population.

National Wilderness Preservation System
■ Wilderness Area
★ Wilderness Area below 25,000 acres

Other Federally Managed Land
■ Bureau of Land Management
■ U.S. Forest Service
■ U.S. Fish and Wildlife Service
■ National Park Service

Puerto Rico

Hawaii

Photo Credits

Front cover: Proposed Browns Canyon Wilderness, Colorado, Courtesy © Jeff Widen

1: Wildlife watching, Katmai National Park and Preserve, Alaska, © Shutterstock

2–3: Sunset, proposed Scotchman Peaks Wilderness, Idaho and Montana, Courtesy © Jim Mellen, Friends of Scotchman Peaks Wilderness, www.scotchmanpeaks.org

4–5: Escalante Canyon, proposed wilderness area within Grand Staircase–Escalante National Monument, Utah, Courtesy © Larry Williams

5: Robert Redford, Courtesy © Kristina Loggia; Grandmother and child, Great Swamp National Wildlife Refuge Wilderness, New Jersey, Courtesy © I. George Bilyk, www.greatswamp.fws.gov

6: Otter Creek Wilderness, West Virginia, Courtesy © Jonathan Jessup, www.jonathanjessup.com

7: Katmai National Park and Preserve, Alaska, © Shutterstock

8 (top): Climber, Organ Pipe National Monument, Arizona, © Shutterstock; (bottom left): Hawaii Volcanoes National Park, Hawaii, © Shutterstock; (bottom right): Moose, Kenai National Wildlife Refuge, Alaska, © Shutterstock

9 (top to bottom): Blueberries, Courtesy © Kendall S. Scott; Rock art, proposed Dominguez Canyon Wilderness, Colorado, Courtesy © Mike Matz; Hikers, King Range Wilderness, California, Courtesy © Bob Wick, Bureau of Land Management

10: Proposed Billy Goat Wilderness, Nevada, Courtesy © Ron Hunter

11 (top to bottom): Wild Sky Wilderness, Washington, Courtesy © Barak Gale, Washington Wilderness Coalition, www.washingtonwilderness.org; Camper, South Dakota grassland, Courtesy © South Dakota Office of Tourism; Barrel cactus, Nevada, Courtesy © Howard Booth; Black Ridge Canyons Wilderness, Colorado and Utah, Courtesy © Jeff Widen; (right) Rock art, proposed Bitter Ridge South Wilderness, Nevada, Courtesy © Kristie Connolly, Nevada Wilderness Project, www.wildnevada.org

12–13: Paria Canyon–Vermillion Cliffs Wilderness, Utah and Arizona, © Shutterstock

12 (inset): Fisherman, proposed Copper Salmon Wilderness, Oregon, Courtesy © Barbara I. Bond, www.barbaraibond.com; www.sportsmenforcoppersalmon.org

14–15: Shi Shi Beach, Olympic National Park, Washington, © Shutterstock

15 (inset): Rock climber, © Shutterstock

16: Proposed Seneca Creek Wilderness, West Virginia, Courtesy © Jonathan Jessup, www.jonathanjessup.com

17 (bottom left): Artist Thomas Paquette, www.thomaspaquette.com, in proposed Cornplanter Wilderness, Allegheny National Forest, Pennsylvania, Courtesy © Kirk Johnson, Friends of the Allegheny Wilderness, www.pawild.org; (upper right): Linville Gorge Wilderness, North Carolina, © Comstock

18–19: Badlands National Park, South Dakota, © Shutterstock

19 (inset): Weminuche Wilderness, Colorado, © Shutterstock

20: Sandia Mountain Wilderness, New Mexico, © Shutterstock; (inset, left): Grizzly, © Comstock; (inset, right): Indian paintbrush, Sandia Mountain Wilderness, New Mexico, © Shutterstock

21: Spawning sockeye salmon, Katmai National Park and Preserve, Alaska, © Shutterstock

22: Prusik Peak, Alpine Lakes Wilderness, Washington, Courtesy © Don Geyer, Mountain Scenes Photography, www.mountainscenes.com

23: Hoh River rain forest, Olympic National Park, Washington, © Shutterstock; (inset): Olympic National Park, Washington, © JupiterImages

24–25: Ragged Top, Ironwood Forest National Monument, Arizona, Courtesy © Murray Bolesta, CactusHuggers Photography, www.cactushuggers.com

24 (inset): Jean Craighead George, Courtesy © High Plains Films, *American Values, American Wilderness*, www.highplainsfilms.org/fp_american.html

25 (inset): Canoe country, Minnesota, Courtesy © Friends of Boundary Waters Wilderness, www.friends-bwca.org

26: Proposed Bitter Ridge South Wilderness, Nevada, Courtesy © Woods Wheatcroft

27 (left): Proposed Badlands Wilderness, Oregon, Courtesy © Mike Stahlberg, *The Register-Guard*; Hiker, Oregon Natural Desert Association, www.onda.org; (right): McGown Peak, Sawtooth Wilderness, Idaho, © Shutterstock

28–29: Isle Royale National Park, Michigan, © Shutterstock

30–31: Weminuche Wilderness, Colorado, © Shutterstock

30 (inset, top): Logan Pass, Glacier National Park, Montana, © Comstock; (inset, bottom): Grand Teton National Park, Wyoming, © Comstock

32: Theodore Roosevelt and John Muir, Yosemite National Park, California, © Bettmann/CORBIS

33 (inset, top): Aldo Leopold, Boundary Waters Canoe Area Wilderness, Minnesota, Courtesy © University of Wisconsin—Madison Archives; (bottom): Butte, © JupiterImages

34–35: Sawtooth Wilderness, Idaho, © Shutterstock

34 (inset, top left): Rocky Mountain Front west of Great Falls, Montana, Courtesy © Lex Hames and Montana Wilderness Association, www.wildmontana.org; (inset, top right): Howard Zahniser, Courtesy © the Zahniser family; (inset bottom left): BLM Wilderness, © Comstock; (inset, bottom right): President Lyndon B. Johnson signing the Wilderness Act, September 3, 1964, Courtesy © National Park Service, Harpers Ferry Center, Historic Graphic Collection, Abbie Rowe, photographer

36–37: Blue Ridge Mountains, Shenandoah National Park, Virginia, © Shutterstock

38–39: © Shutterstock

38 (inset): Nancy Hall, proposed wilderness in Gold Butte region of southeastern Nevada, Nevada Wilderness Project, www.wildnevada.org, Courtesy © Woods Wheatcroft

39 (inset, top): Guadalupe Mountains National Park, Texas, © Shutterstock; (inset, bottom): Idaho Wheelers for Wilderness in front of US Capitol, Courtesy © US Representative Mike Simpson

40–41: Ruby Beach, Olympic National Park, Washington, © Shutterstock

42–43: Denali National Park and Preserve, Alaska, © Shutterstock

44: Denali National Park and Preserve, Alaska, © Shutterstock

45: Katmai National Park and Preserve, Alaska, © Shutterstock

46–47: Stellar sea lions, © Shutterstock

46 (inset): President Jimmy and Rosalynn Carter, proposed wilderness on the

For Further Information

Books

Scott, Doug. *The Enduring Wilderness: Protecting Our Heritage through the Wilderness Act.* Foreword by Theodore Roosevelt IV. Golden, CO: Fulcrum Publishing, 2004.

Accessible primer on all aspects of wilderness preservation—history, policy, administration, international- and state-level wilderness protection. Includes full notes and complete text of the Wilderness Act.

A must for ordinary citizens who care about saving our wilderness heritage for future generations. Hopeful, practical, and compelling.
　　　　　　　　　—Christopher Reeve

Nash, Roderick. *Wilderness and the American Mind*, 4th ed. New Haven, CT: Yale University Press, 2001.

The definitive intellectual history of the wilderness idea; a classic in environmental history.

One of those rare works that combines exemplary scholarship with readability.
　　　　　　　—**Washington Post Book World**

On the Web

www.leaveitwild.org

Up-to-the-minute information on what is happening in wilderness preservation, nationally and in your own state, from the Campaign for America's Wilderness. Reports status of all pending wilderness protection legislation in Congress and links for contacting leading wilderness protection and outings groups in your state.

www.wilderness.net

The definitive site for information on the National Wilderness Preservation System and on each of the more than seven hundred wilderness areas designated by Congress, including information on planning your visit. Continually updated, this is a joint project of the University of Montana and the four federal agencies that administer our wilderness areas.

About the Campaign for America's Wilderness

The Campaign for America's Wilderness works with state and local citizen groups across the country to help them achieve statutory protection through the Wilderness Act for treasured places on federal lands. These efforts are positive and proactive, working in collaboration with many other local, state, and national partner organizations.

Acknowledgments

While this is a Campaign for America's Wilderness book, the opinions expressed are my own. We have assigned all royalties to support the citizen activism that protects wilderness. I am grateful to the photographers who generously donated their artistry to this book, to Robert Redford and Joyce Deep, and to those in conservation groups and federal agencies who have contributed to my understanding of this work.

The family I've found at Fulcrum Publishing goes beyond any author's fondest dream—Bob and Charlotte Baron, Sam Scinta, gifted editor Faith Marcovecchio, and talented designer Jack Lenzo.

My hat is off, most of all, to the legions of ordinary Americans who choose to "practice democracy" by marshalling the unrivaled citizen power available to all of us to gain protection of our wilderness—America's common ground. Join us!